Level Five
E/Grade 3

JOHN W. SCHAUM Presents

AMERICAN SONATINAS

SIX ORIGINAL SONATINAS BY SIX AMERICAN COMPOSERS

FOREWORD

In presenting this collection of sonatinas by American composers, the aim is to provide material that meets the requirements of an original American composition suitable for auditions, competitions and recitals. All the composers are American by birth or naturalization. All are musicians of the highest calibre.

Each sonatina is prefaced by brief biographical comments accompanied by an artist's sketch of the composer. The form and analysis of each sonatina is outlined by inserting Roman numerals at the start of the various sections. The sections are described in footnotes at the bottom page of each movement.

The sonatinas occur in progressive order according to the degree of difficulty.

SCHAUM PUBLICATIONS, INC.
10235 N. Port Washington Rd. - Mequon, WI 53092

07-05
AK-17

The Sonatina Story

A sonatina is a small sonata consisting of one, two, or three movements each one shorter and less elaborated, or developed than in the sonata. The structure of the sonatina is not as strict in form as the sonata. Three of the sonatinas in this collection are one movement in length: *Pilgrim Sonatina, Colonial Sonatina,* and *Spinning Wheel Sonatina.* The others are written in three movements. When a sonatina is made up of three movements, the first is usually the most technical; the second movement is generally slower in speed and more expressive; the third is customarily in a light carefree mood. All six of the sonatinas are in the classical tradition. For example, Engelmann indicated in his notes that his sonatina was *á la Haydn,* meaning in the style and tradition of Haydn.

Many of the master composers, such as Haydn, Mozart, and Beethoven wrote sonatinas as well as sonatas. There is even a modern concert sonatina by Ravel which is extremely virtuosic in character and technically very difficult. A host of other composers wrote compositions in the sonatina form. Among the foremost are Clementi, Kuhlau, Diabelli, Reinecke, and Lichner, to mention a few. Many of their works are deservedly in the piano teaching repertoire today.

Contents

Pilgrim Sonatina

Edward Holyoke Holst emigrated to America in 1874. He was born in Copenhagen, Denmark in 1843. His versatile career included acting, dance instructing, playwrighting as well as composing and conducting. His music is light in character displaying great melodic sensitivity. He wrote more than 2,000 numbers including compositions for military band, a comic opera, and many piano pieces.

EDWARD HOLST
(1843 - 1899)

* I = First Theme; II = Bridge Passage; III = Second Theme; IV = Bridge Passage; V = First Theme.

f
Andante moderato (M.M. ♩=104)
II
p
III
mf
piu mosso
p
IV
pp
rit

Tempo I
mf
p
mf
p
mf
f
rit.

Colonial Sonatina

Although Hans Engelmann was of German birth his career and music are thoroughly American. Born in Berlin on June 16, 1872, he came to the United States in 1891 where he spent the rest of his life. He composed over three thousand piano pieces including the world famous *Melody of Love*. He was prominent as a conductor, composer and pianist.

H. ENGELMANN Op. 372 No. 12
(1872 - 1914)

* I = First Theme; II = Development of First Theme; III = Second Theme; IV = Bridge Passage; V = Second Theme; VI = Bridge Passage; VII First Theme; VIII = Coda.

p
III
pp
delicato
cresc.
pp
IV
p
cresc.

rit.
V
a tempo
energico
VI
VII
p grazioso

mf
marc.
p
VIII
f
p
mf
f
rit.

Spirit of '76 Sonatina

In the year 1858, on the sixteenth of May, Frank Lynes was born in Cambridge, Massachusetts. His musical training was acquired at the New England Conservatory in Boston where Benjamin Lang instructed him in piano and organ. John K. Paine was his harmony teacher. His career consisted of many musical activities: pianist, organist, teacher, conductor and composer. He wrote chamber music, piano pieces, part songs and vocal solos.

FRANK LYNES, Op. 39, No. 1
(1858 - 1914)

* I= First Theme; II= Bridge Passage; III= First Theme; IV= Coda.

III
p
mf
dim.
IV
mf

Minuet (Allegretto) (M.M. ♩=108)

* I=First Theme; II=Second Theme; III=First Theme.

mf
III
cresc.
f
p
mf

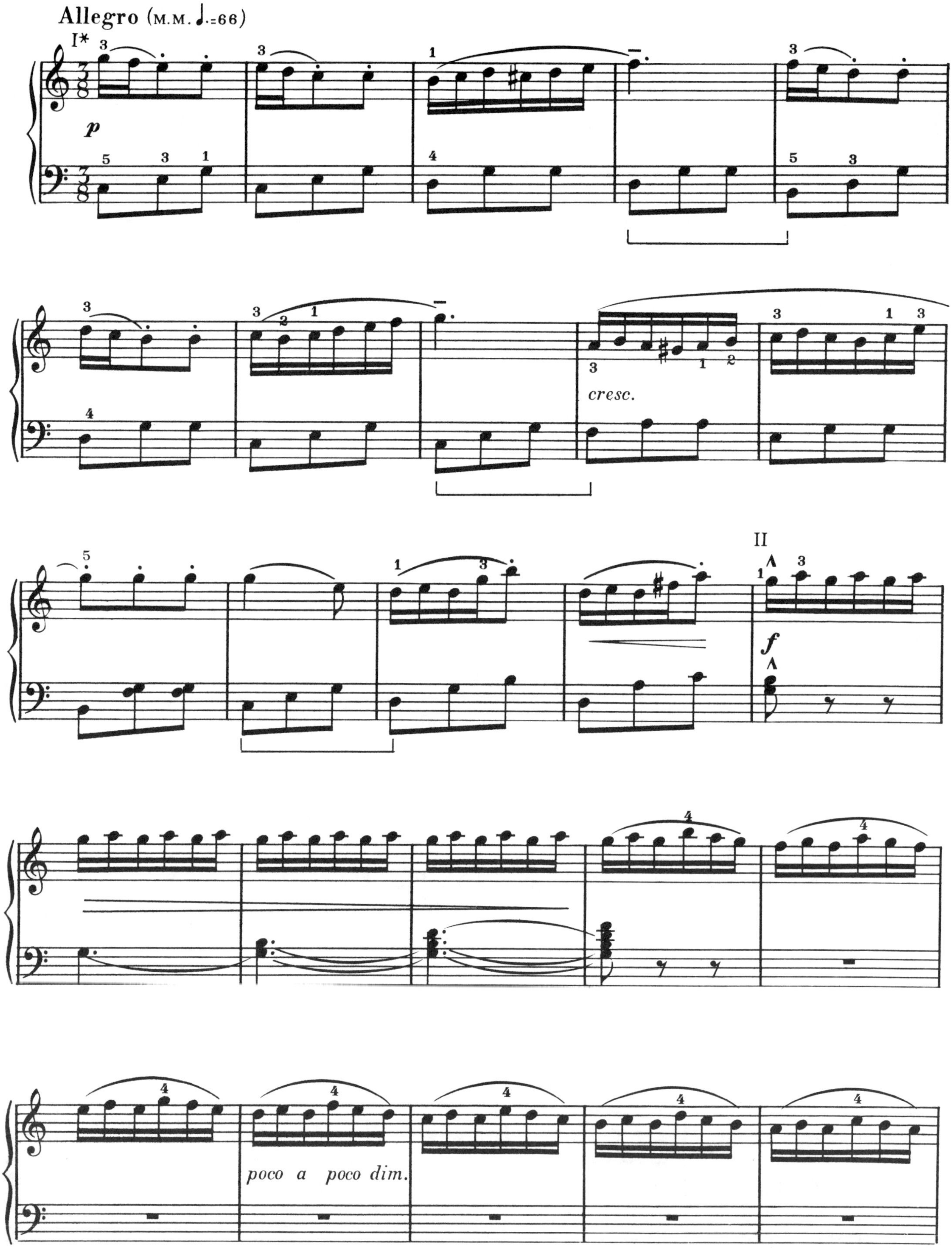

* I=First Theme; II=Bridge Passage; III=First Theme; IV=Coda.

III
p
cresc.
IV

New England Sonatina

In 1859, Frank Addison Porter was born in Dixmont, Maine. He became a graduate of the New England Conservatory in Boston in 1884. His career centered around this venerable music school. He was appointed professor of piano in 1885 and in 1892 he was promoted to head of the piano department, a post which he held for thirty years. He composed a great deal of piano music during this period.

F. ADDISON PORTER
(1859-1941)

* I=First Theme; II=Second Theme; III=Development of First Theme; IV=Bridge Passage; V=First Theme; VI=Second Theme (in tonic key.)

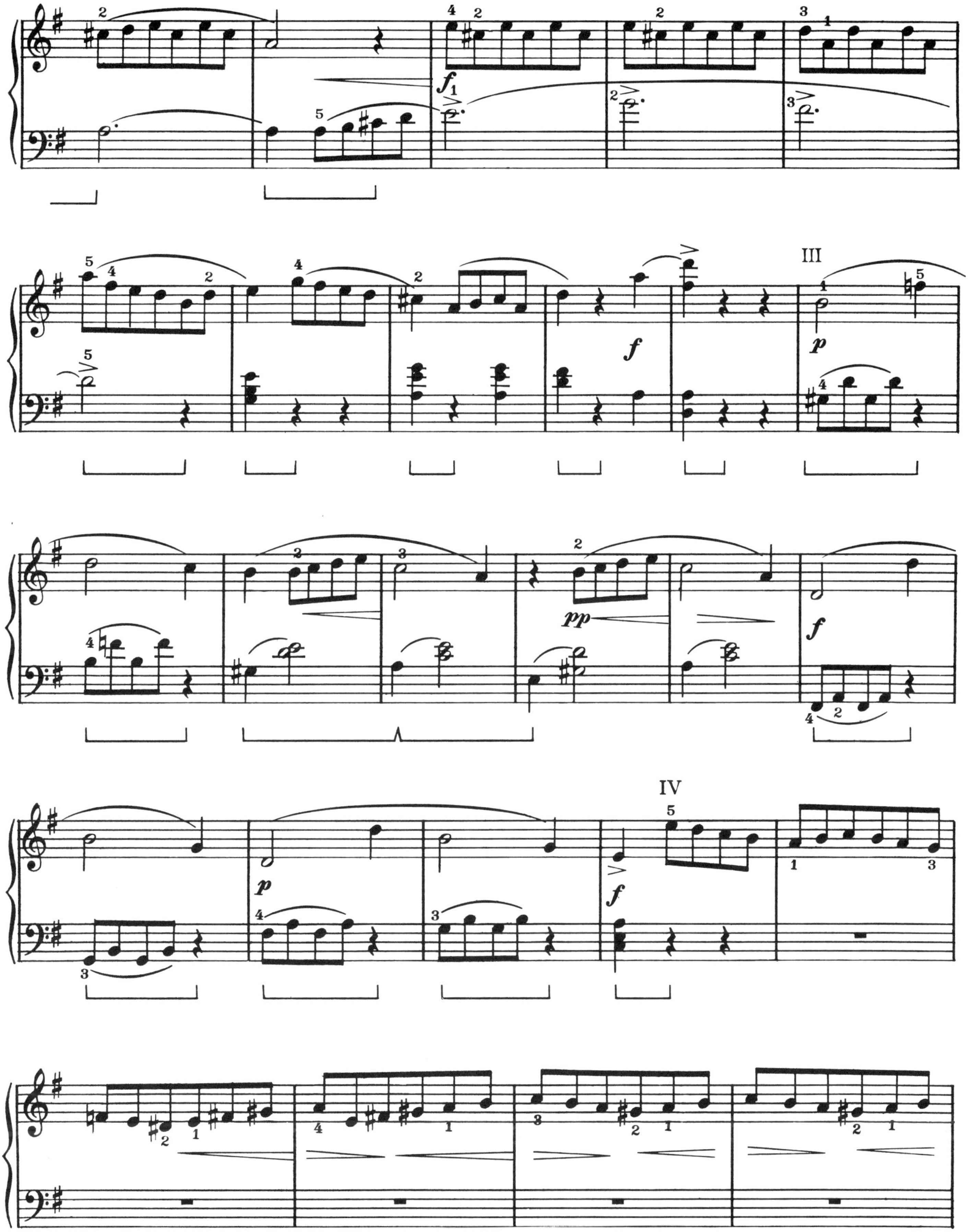
III
IV

p
f
p rit.
f a tempo
V
ff
mf
f
VI
f
mf

Andante (M.M. ♪=116)

*I = First Theme; II = Second Theme; III = First Theme; IV = Coda.

Allegretto (M.M. ♩. = 112)

*I = First Theme; II = Second Theme; III = First Theme; IV = Coda.

II
cresc.
III

f
f
ff
IV
f
mf
dim.
rit.
f
a tempo

Rustic Sonatina

William Dawson Armstrong was born in Alton, Illinois on February 11, 1868. He studied piano and composition in St. Louis under Ernest Kroeger. In Chicago, he mastered the organ under the tutelage of Clarence Eddy. He was the solo organist at the St. Louis World Fair. In 1908, he opened his own music school in Alton, Illinois. His compositions include an opera, an orchestral suite, an overture and numerous vocal and piano pieces.

Wm. D. ARMSTRONG
(1868-1936)

Allegro (M.M. ♩=108)

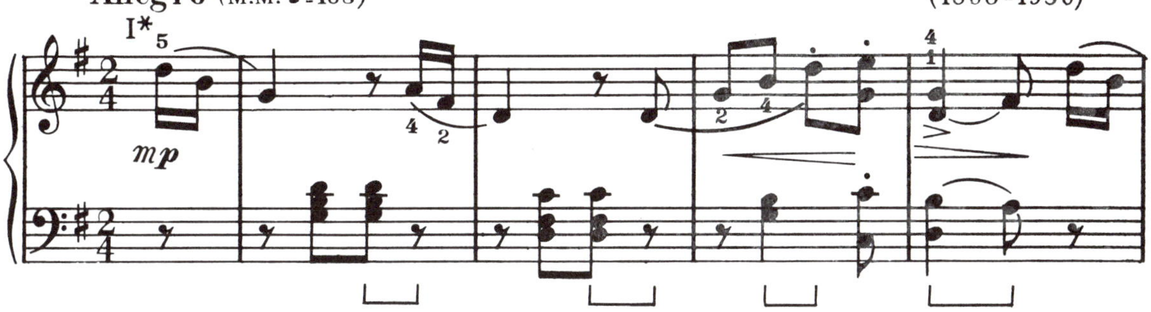

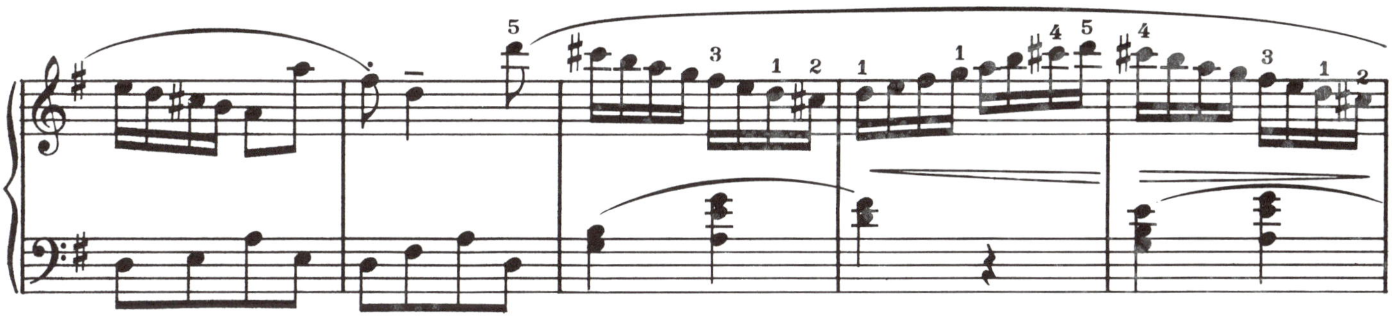

* I=First Theme; II=Second Theme; III=Development of First Theme; IV=Development of Second Theme; V=First Theme; VI=Second Theme (Tonic key); VII=Coda.

IV
cresc.
fz
V
mp
a tempo
VI
VII
f
p

* I = First Theme; II = Second Theme; III = First Theme.

*I=First Theme; II=Second Theme; III=First Theme; IV=Coda.

III
f
a tempo
p
f
p
IV
2 3 1
f
8va
2 1
p
16va
2 1
pp
8va
f

Spinning Wheel Sonatina

The birthplace of Frederick Newell Shackley was Laconia, New Hampshire; his birthdate was October 25, 1868. He studied at the New England Conservatory and made Boston his home. Here he became a church organist, choral conductor and piano teacher. He composed cantatas, church music, piano and organ pieces.

FREDERICK N. SHACKLEY
(1868 - 1937)

* I= First Theme; II= Second Theme; III= Development; IV=First Theme; V=Second Theme (Tonic key).

p
pp
mf
III

cresc.
dim.
8va
cresc.
8va
IV

8va
cresc.
p
pp
mf
f
rit.

Successful Schaum Sheet Music

This is a Partial List — Showing Level 5 through Level 7

• = Original Form ✓ = Chord Symbols

ANIMALS

LEVEL

67-23 • OF A TAILOR AND A BEAR .... *MacDowell* 6
67-03 WHISTLER AND HIS DOG .... *Pryor* 6

BOOGIE

64-06 COTTON PICKIN' BOOGIE .... *Myddleton* 5
67-21 • DEEP RHYTHM (Boogie Style) .... *Reisfeld* 6
64-29 IN THE HALL of the BOOGIE KING .... *Grieg/Schaum* 5

CHRISTMAS

70-11 CAROL of the BELLS .... *Ukranian Bell Carol* 6
70-03 CHRISTMAS FANTASY .... *Medley* 6
67-02 GREENSLEEVES (6/8 Time) .... *Cameo Transcription* 6
67-15 I WONDER AS I WANDER .... *Appalachian Carol* 6
70-04 JINGLE BELLS JUBILEE .... *Theme & Variations* 6
67-18 RISE UP SHEPHERDS, AND FOLLOW .... *Spiritual* 6
67-06 TOYLAND .... *Herbert* 6

CIRCUS

64-36 CIRCUS GRAND MARCH ("Entry of the Gladiators") .... *Fucik* 5

CLASSICS

67-16 • *Bach* .... COMPUTER INVENTION (2-Part, No. 13) 6
64-05 *Chopin* .... ETUDE IN E MAJOR 5
67-20 *Clementi* .... CONVERSATION WALTZ 6
69-02 *Dvorak* .... HUMORESQUE (Concert Transcription) 7
64-04 *Handel* .... HALLELUJAH CHORUS 5
64-16 • *Heller* .... CURIOUS STORY 5
67-10 *Liszt* .... FORGOTTEN WALTZ 6
67-17 *Pachelbel* .... CANON 6
67-01 *Rossini* .... LA DANZA (6/8 Time) 6
64-02 *Saint-Saens* .... DANSE MACABRE 5
67-07 *Schubert* .... AVE MARIA (Cameo Transcription) 6
64-09 ✓ *Strauss* .... BLUE DANUBE 5
64-35 *Tchaikowsky* .... MARCH from 6th SYMPHONY (3rd Mvt) 5

COUNTRY/WESTERN

64-27 • HOEDOWN (Triplets) .... *Leach* 5

DESCRIPTIVE MUSIC

64-22 • REFLECTIONS .... *Cahn* 5
64-23 STORM, The (Minor Key) .... *Pitcher* 5
64-31 • SUMMER NOCTURNE .... *Levin* 5
64-24 • TWO MOODS (Major - Minor) .... *Cahn* 5
64-08 VALSE TRISTE (Minor Key) .... *Sibelius* 5
64-30 • VIENNA REMEMBERED .... *Cahn* 5

DISSONANCE

67-14 • SOUVENIR (Quartal-Quintal Harmony) .... *Croom* 6
64-20 • TOKEN (Quartal-Quintal Harmony) .... *Croom* 5

DUETS (1 Piano, 4 Hands)

LEVEL

71-06 BEETHOVEN'S 6th SYMPHONY .... *(2nd Mvt. Theme)* 5
71-04 RONDO IN A MAJOR, Op. 107 .... *Schubert* 5
71-05 SLAVONIC DANCE in E-Minor, Op. 72 .... *Dvorak* 6

FLOWERS

64-03 • CORSAGE WALTZ .... *Schaum* 5
64-28 • GENTLE BLOSSOM .... *Cahn* 5

JAZZ STYLE

67-24 BLUE VELVET .... *Hudson* 6
64-15 • CLOWNING AROUND .... *King* 5
64-38 • ROCK RHAPSODY (Syncopated 3/4 Time) .... *King* 5
64-37 • SNAZZY .... *Weston* 5

LATIN AMERICAN

67-22 • FIESTA EN ESPANA (Minor Key) .... *Cahn* 6
69-01 MEXICAN HAT DANCE .... *Concert Transcription* 7

MARCHES

67-05 MARCH of the TOYS (Grace Notes) .... *Herbert* 6

MINOR KEY

64-34 • CONTEMPLATION .... *Cahn* 5

RAGTIME

64-25 ✓ ALEXANDER'S RAGTIME BAND .... *Berlin* 5

ROMANTIC MOOD

67-08 CLAIR DE LUNE (Key of C Major) .... *Debussy* 6
64-10 • HAWAIIAN NOCTURNE .... *Weston* 5
67-09 KISS ME AGAIN .... *Herbert* 6
64-12 ORIENTAL NOCTURNE .... *Borodin* 5
64-22 • REFLECTIONS .... *Cahn* 5
64-32 • ROMANCE .... *Levin* 5
64-33 SERENADE .... *Herbert* 5
64-31 • SUMMER NOCTURNE .... *Levin* 5

SHOWY DISPLAY SOLOS

64-13 • AVALANCHE .... *Heller* 5
67-12 FIREWORKS (Grace Notes) .... *Ponchielli* 6
64-14 MUSICAL JEWEL BOX (Both Hands in Treble) .... *Heins* 5
64-39 • POWERHOUSE .... *Schaum* 5
67-11 • SOLFEGGIETTO .... *C.P.E. Bach* 6

SONATINA

64-26 • RUSTIC SONATINA .... *Armstrong* 5

TV THEME

67-19 TRUMPET FANFARE (used in "Masterpiece Theater") 6